ROGER SESSIONS
Second String Quartet

Score

$4⁰⁰

Edward B. Marks Music Corporation
136 West 52nd Street • New York, N.Y. 10019

SECOND STRING Q

P̶ᵖ̶ - *principal voice*
S̶ᵖ̶ - *secondary voice*
*tr̶ — above the note indicates a trill
with a tone (or semitone) above, as indicated;
below the note, with a tone or semitone below.*

I.

ROGER SESSIONS

Printed in U.S.A.

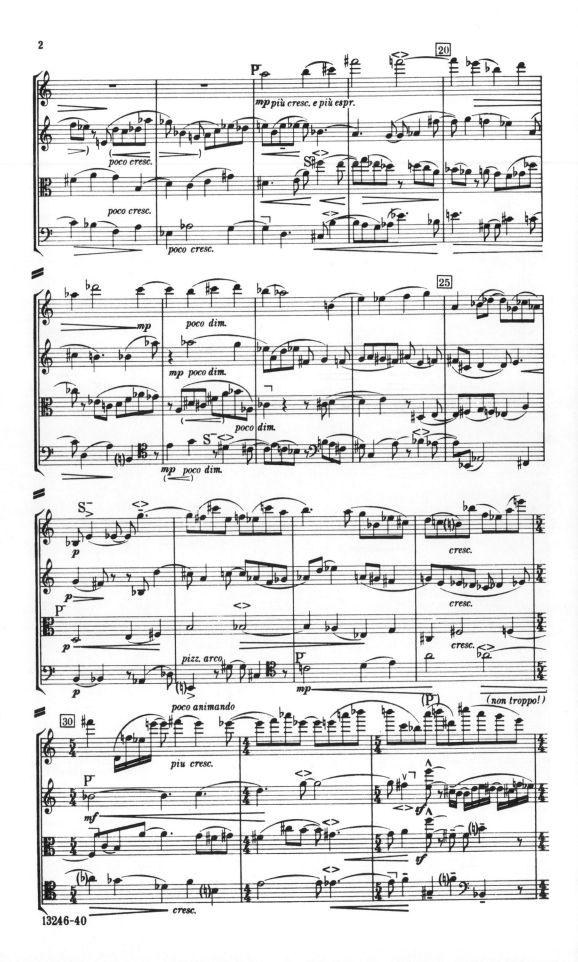

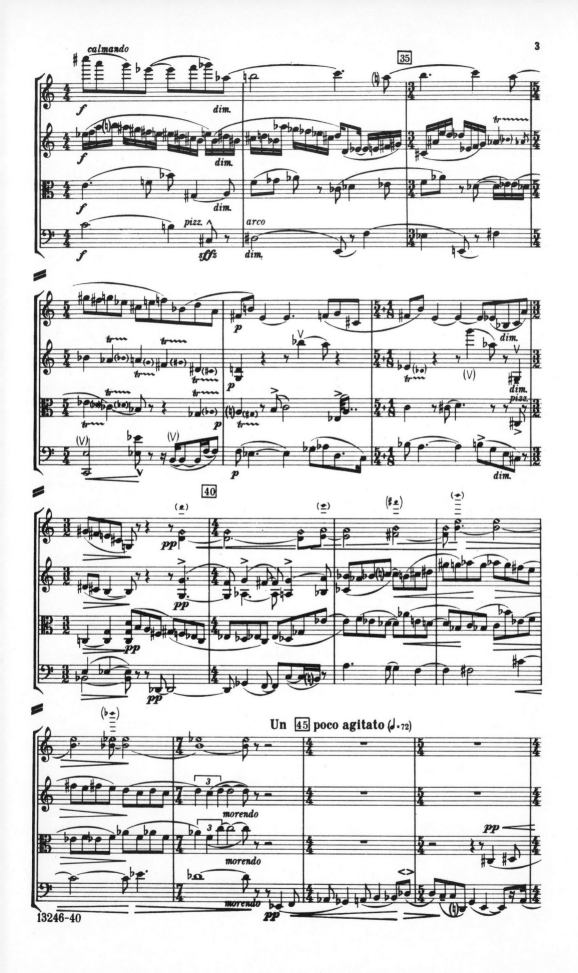

pp poco cresc.
poco cresc.
poco cresc.
dim.
50
cresc.
mf
cresc.
cresc.
poco animando
poco a poco calmando
dim. poco a poco
poco meno f
55

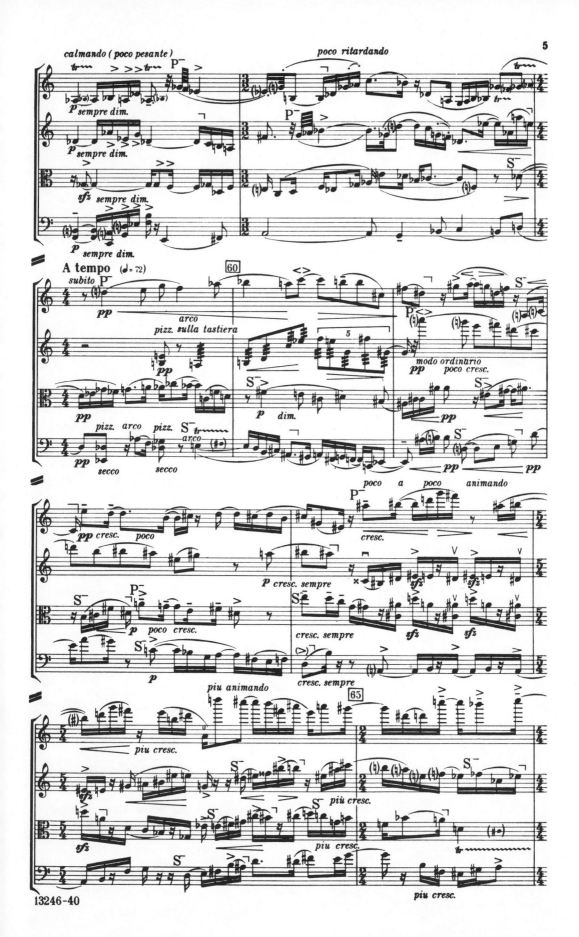

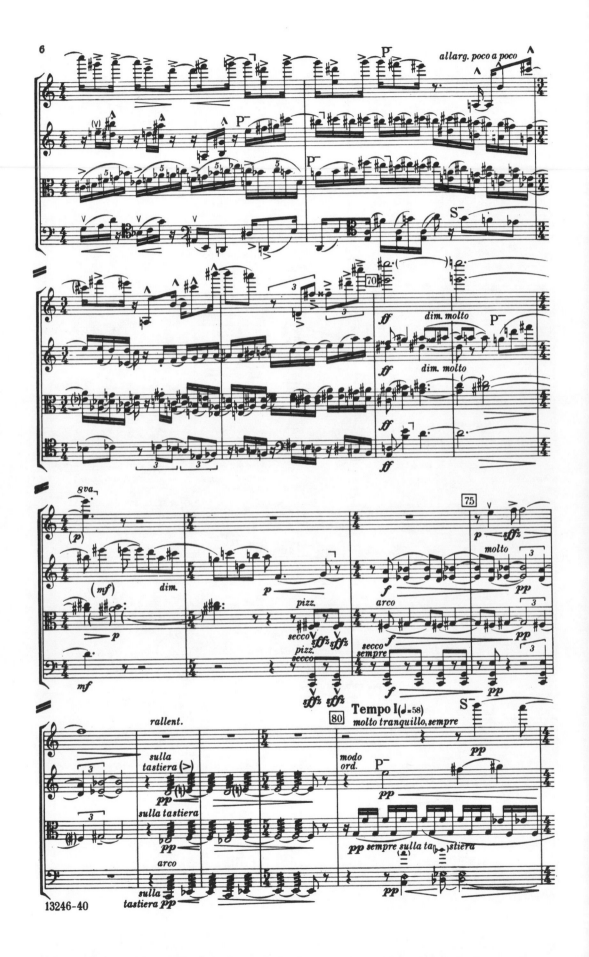

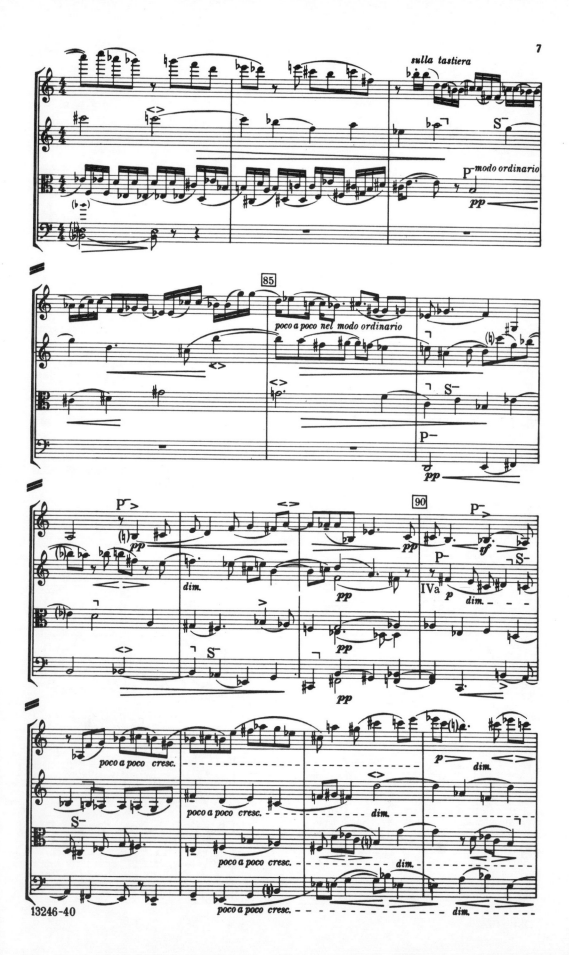

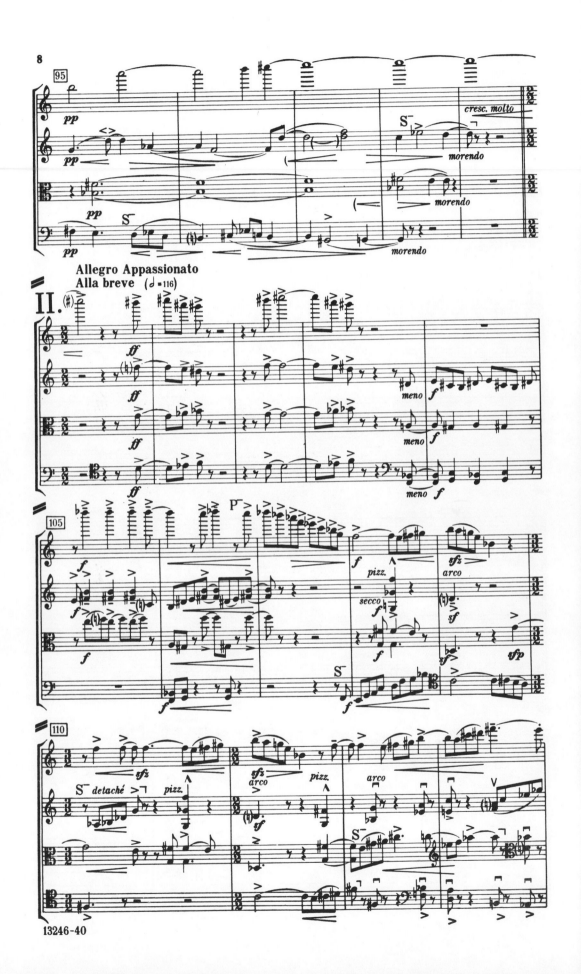

Allegro Appassionato
Alla breve (♩ = 116)

II.

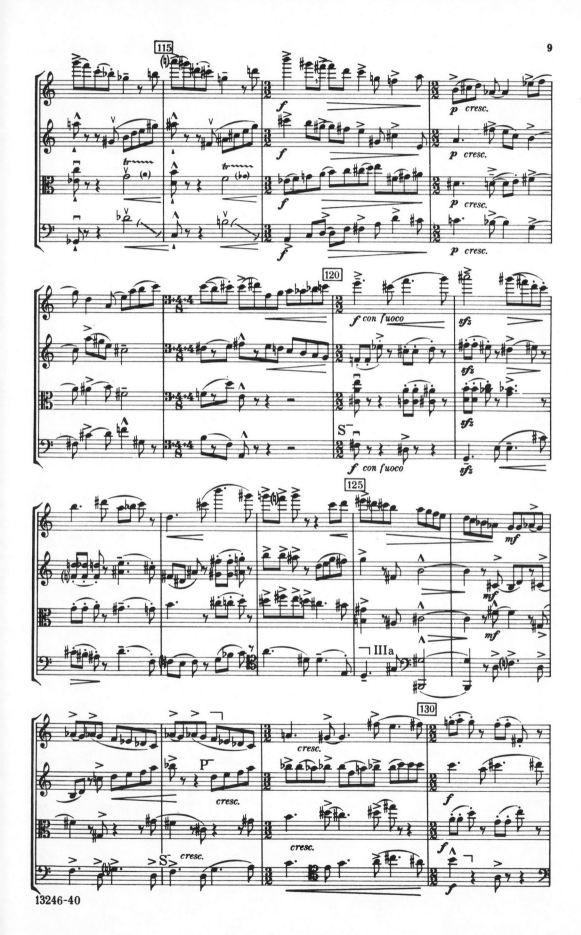

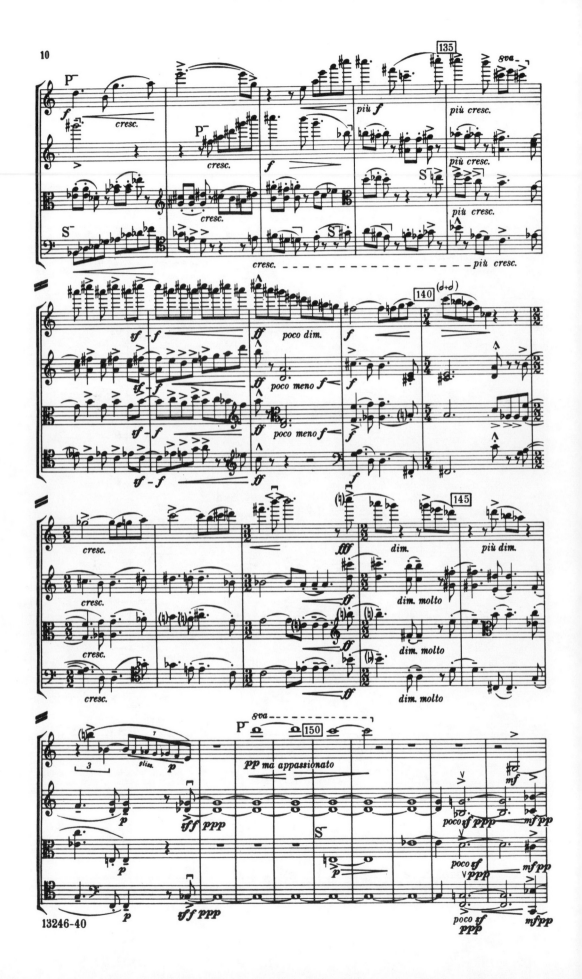

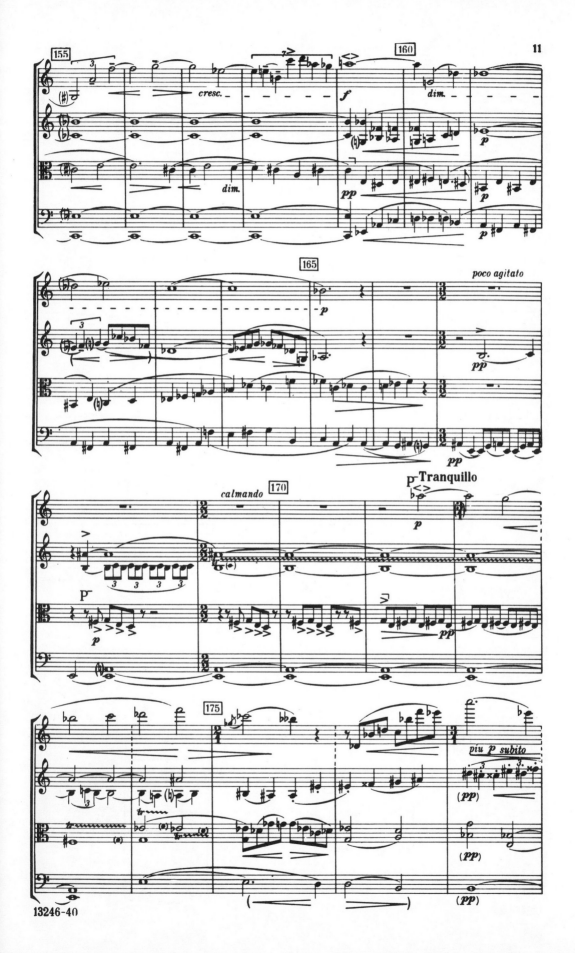

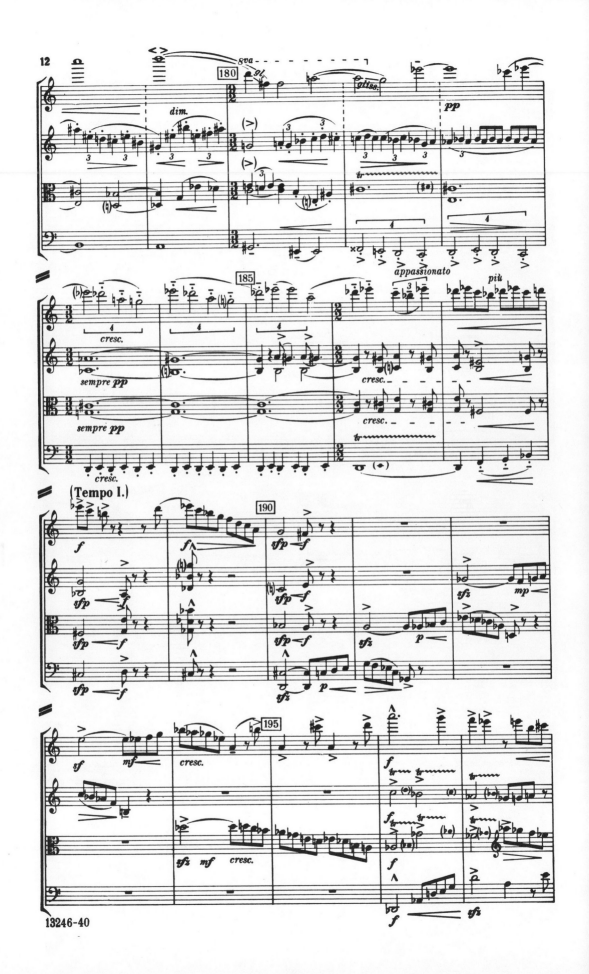

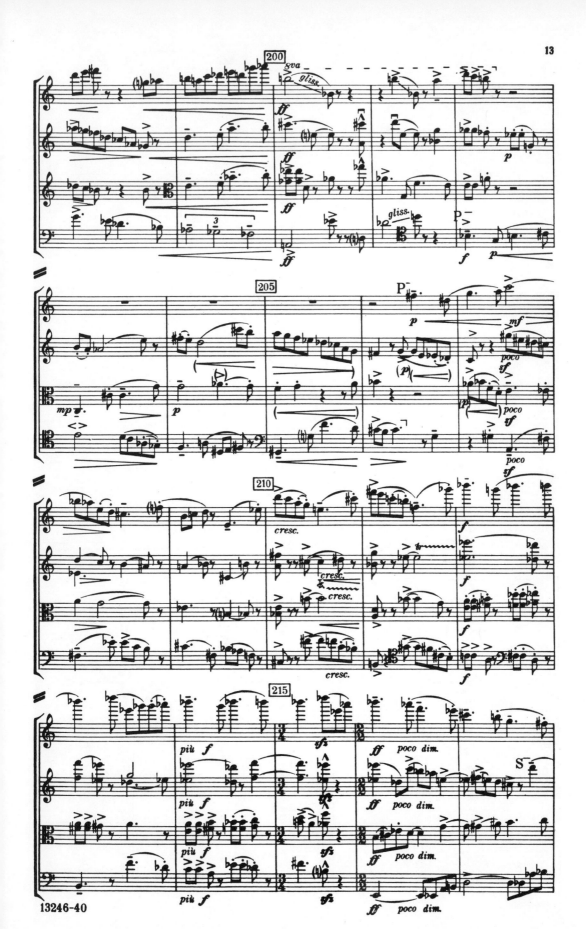

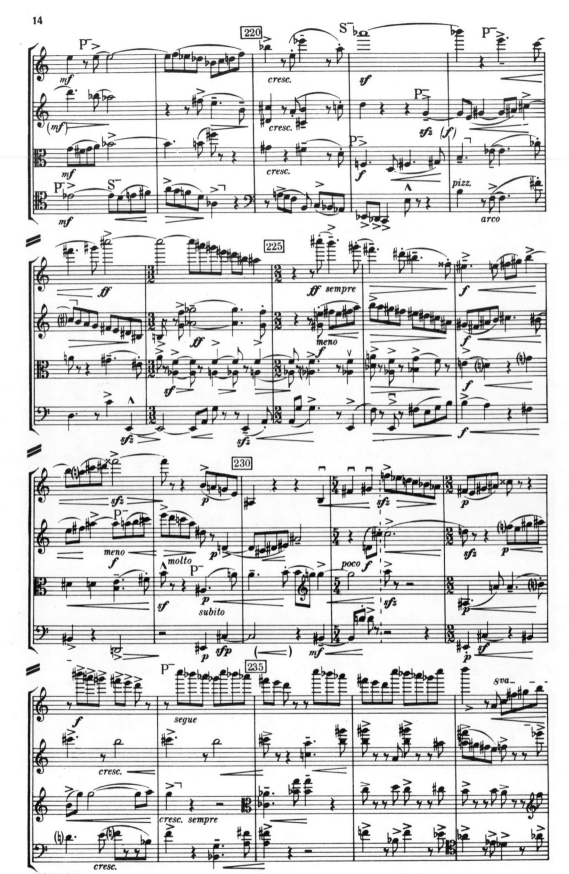

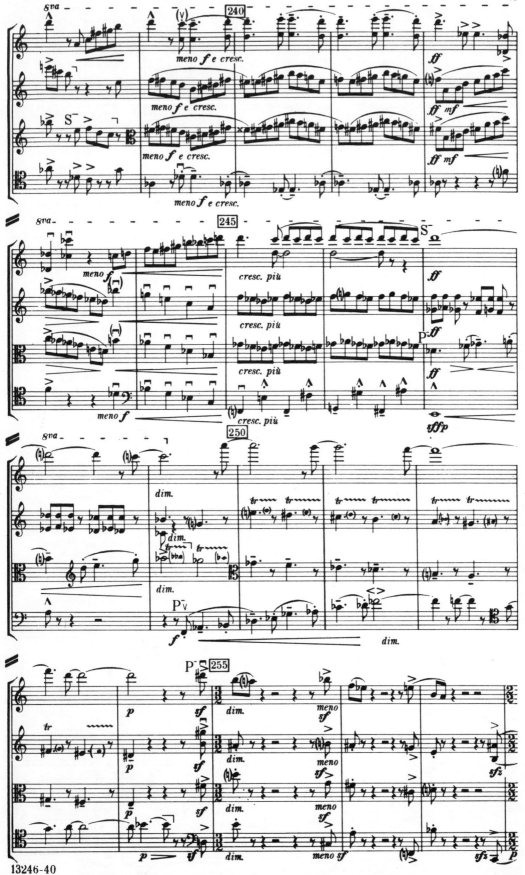

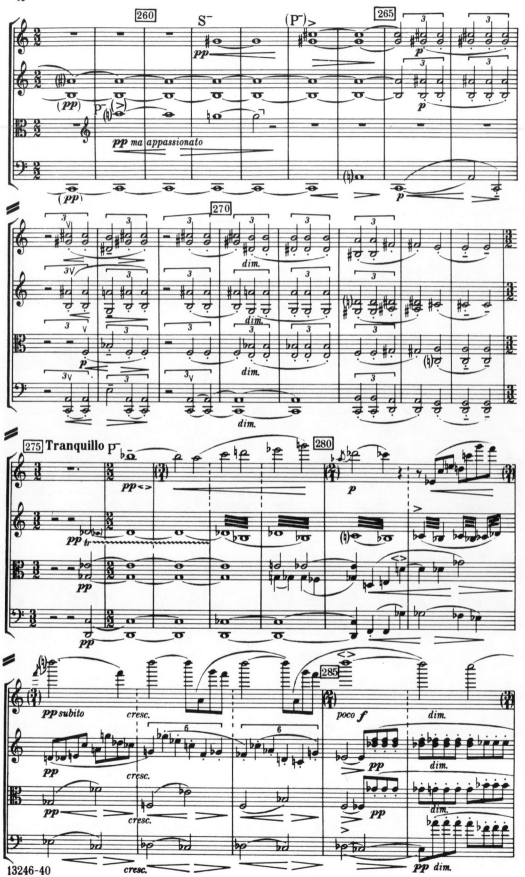

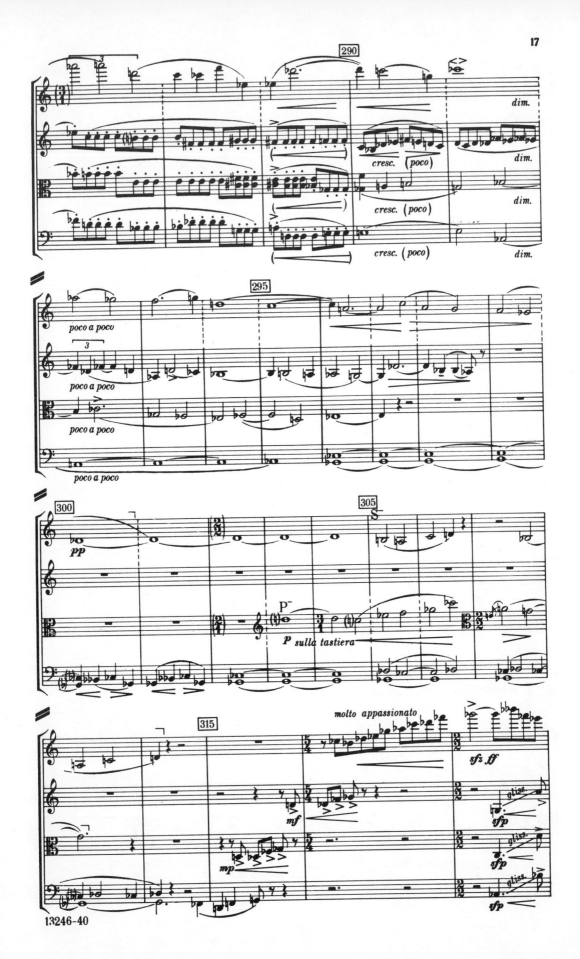

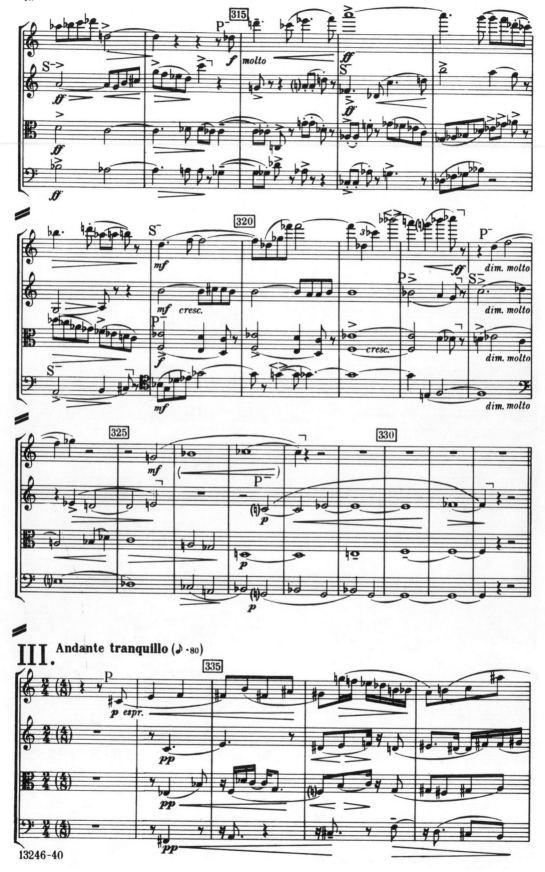

III. Andante tranquillo (♪ = 80)

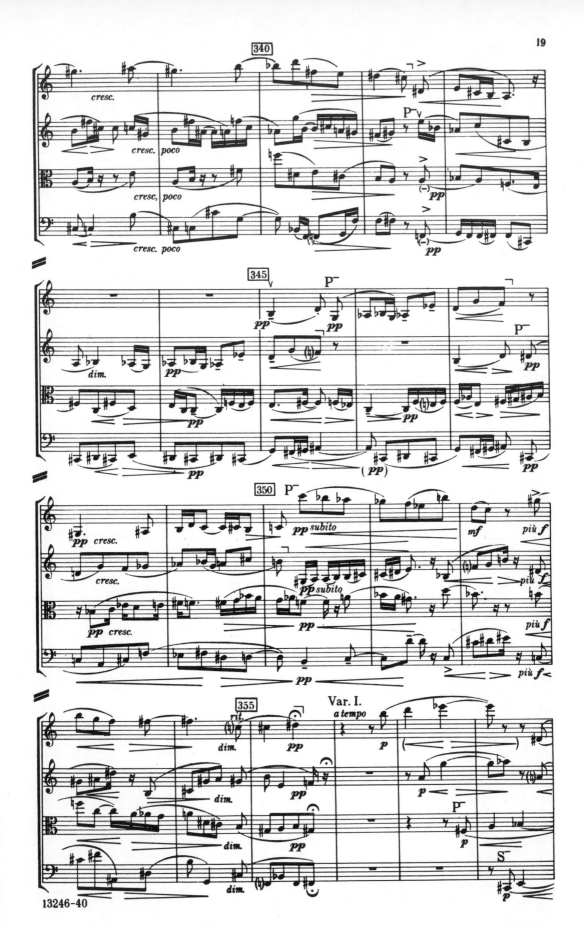

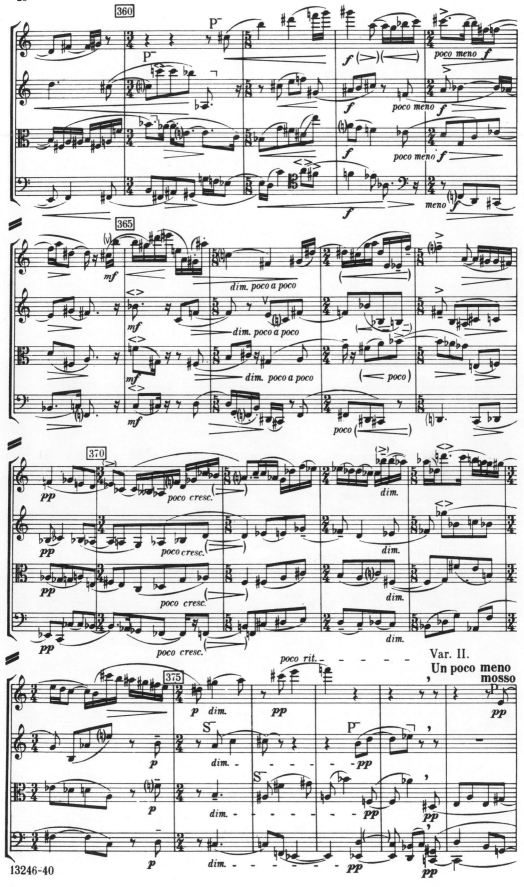

e sostenuto (♪=69)

tranquillo molto

Var. III.(♪=60)
Adagio molto

*⟲let string strike sharply against fingerboard

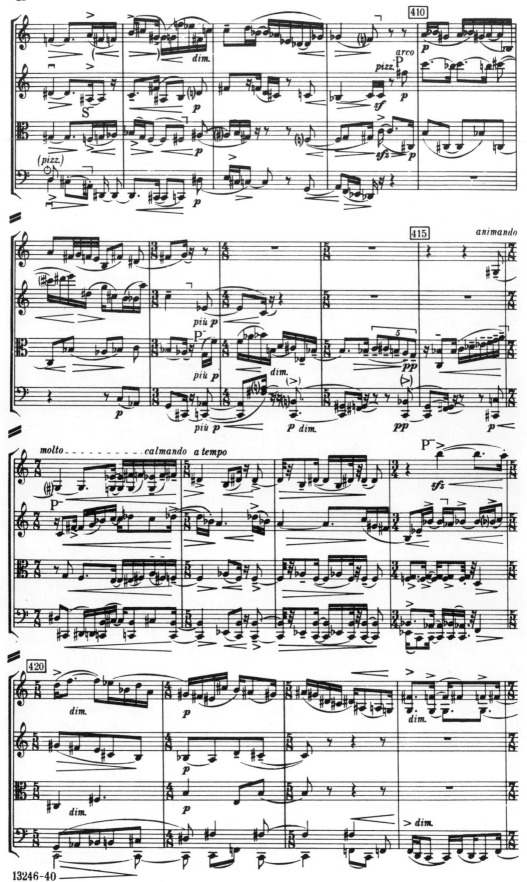

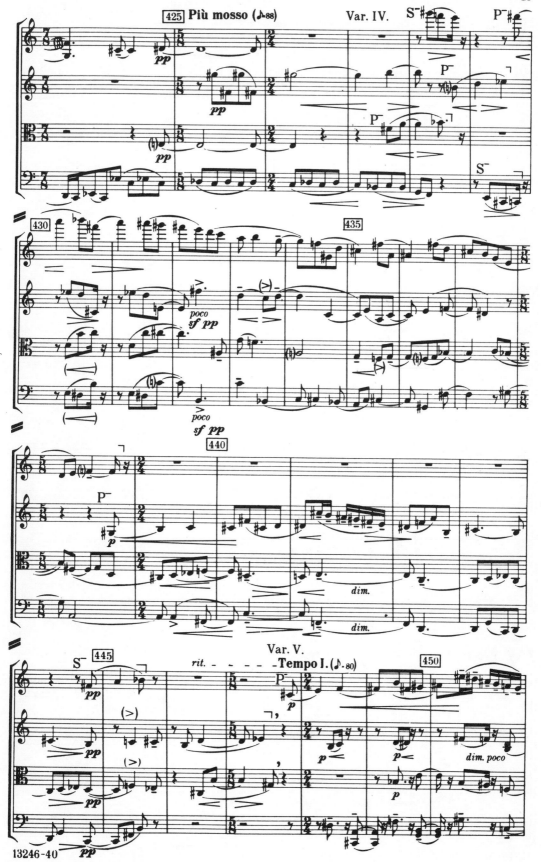

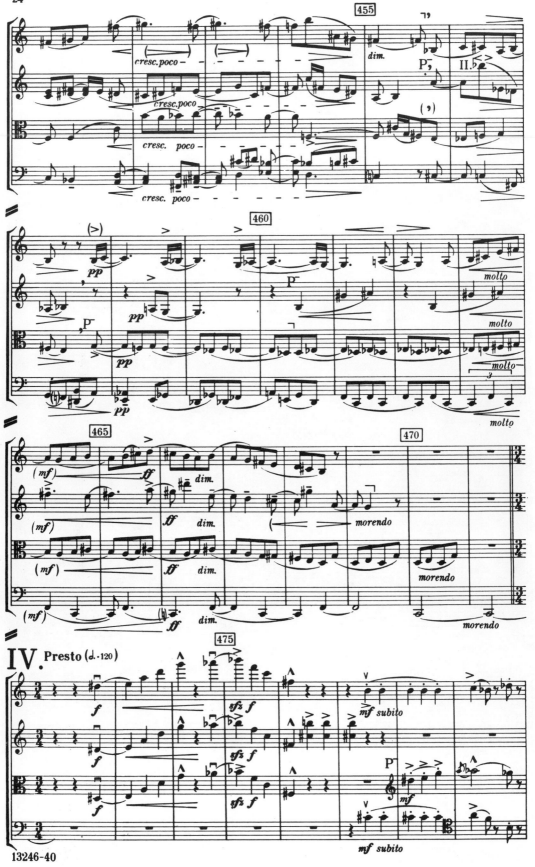

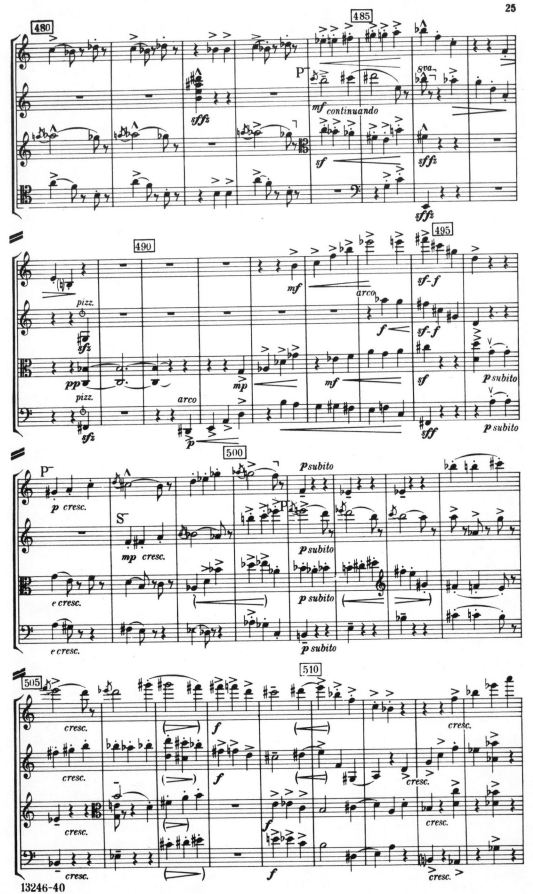

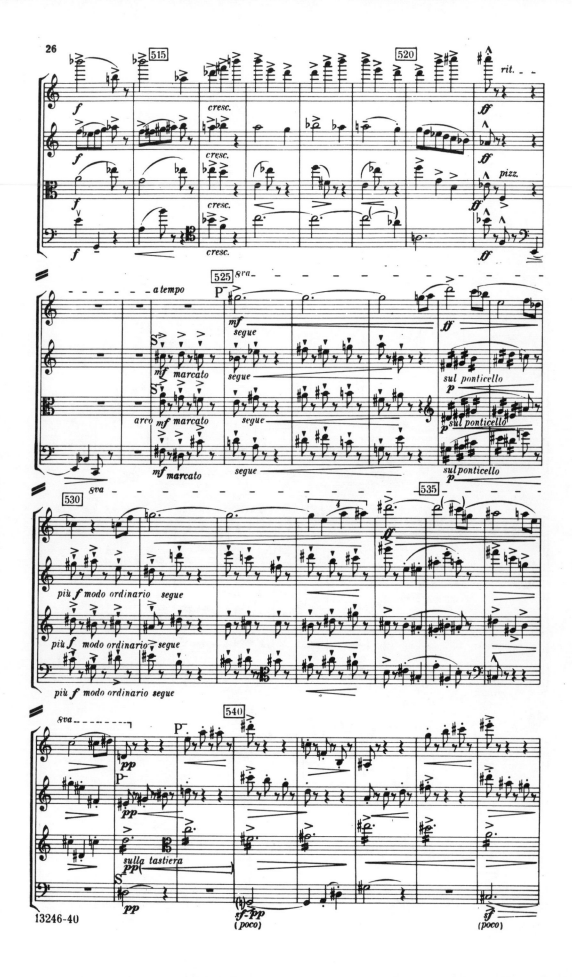

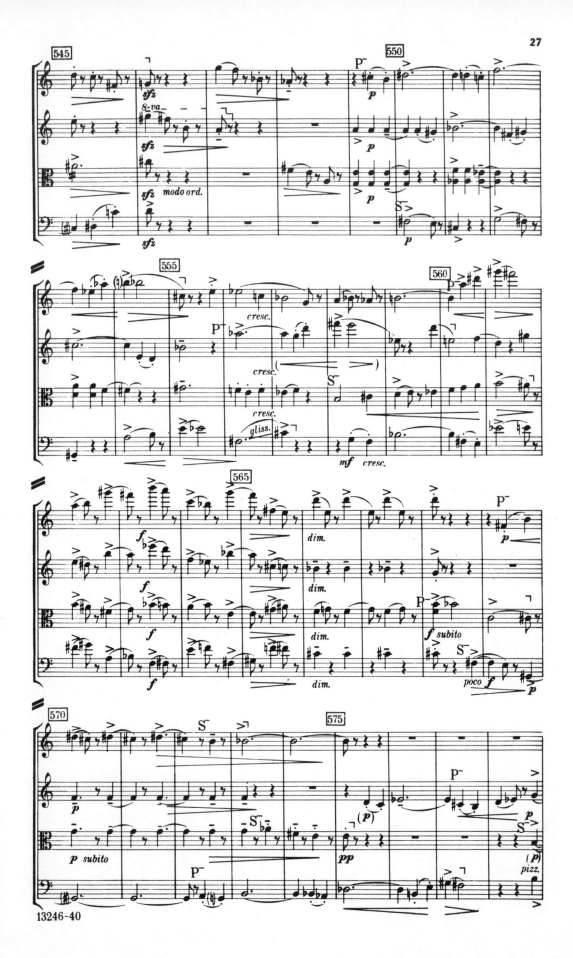

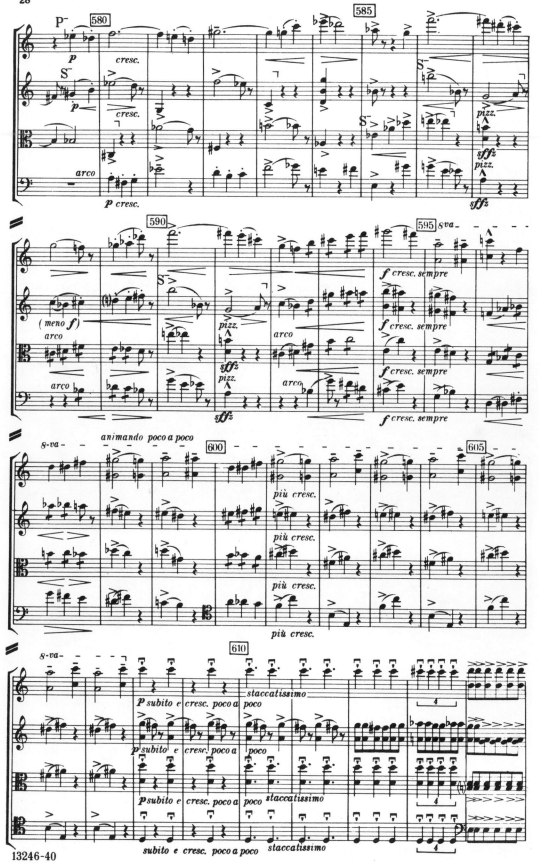

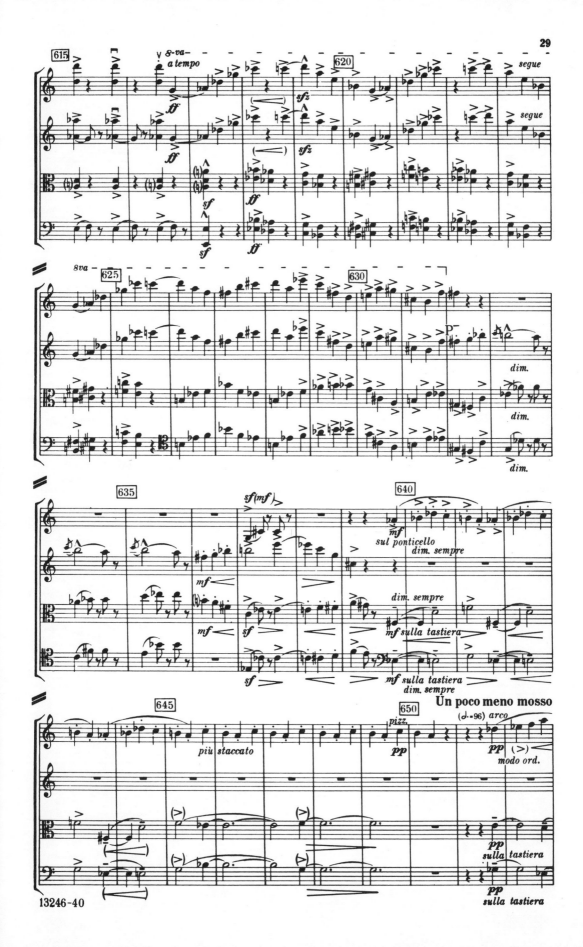

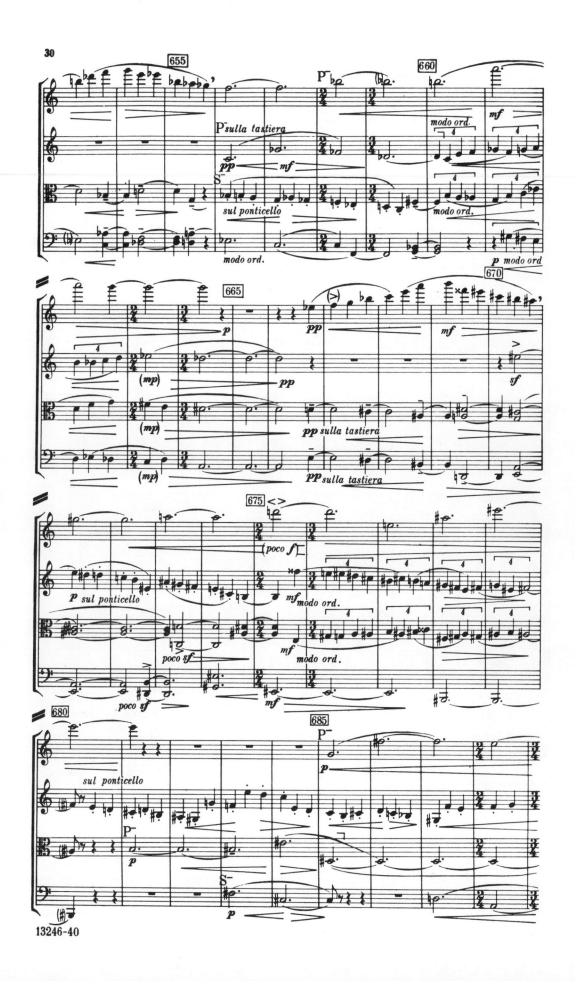

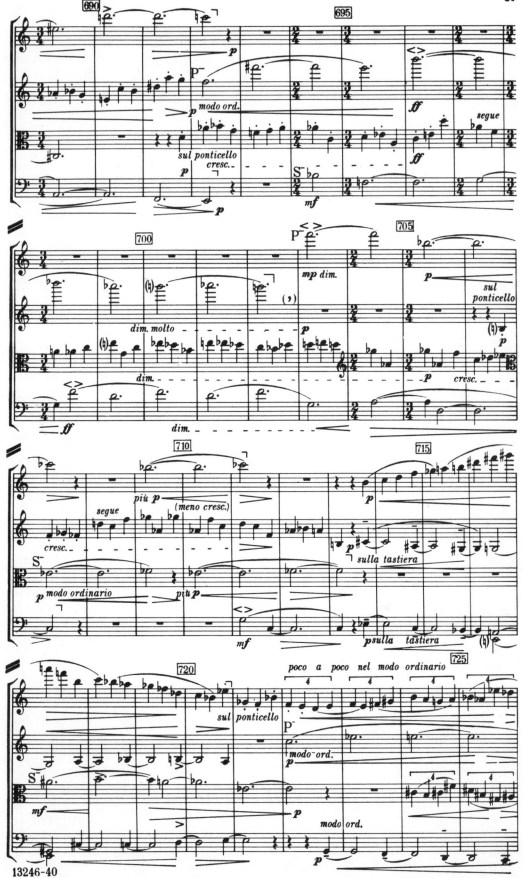

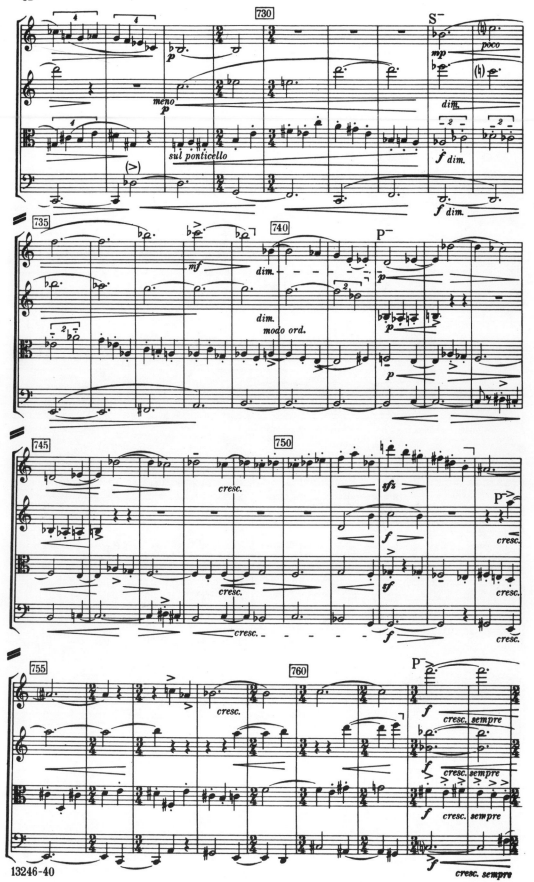

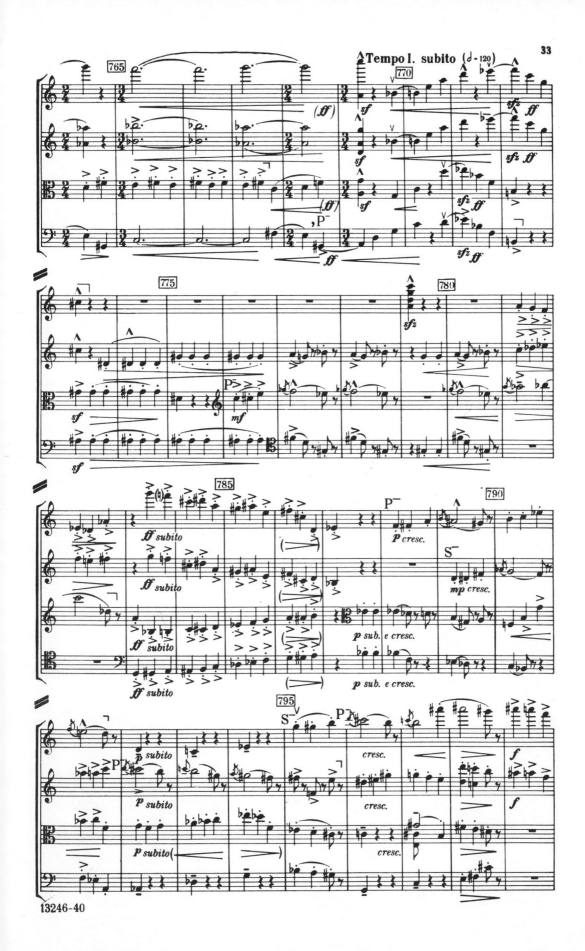

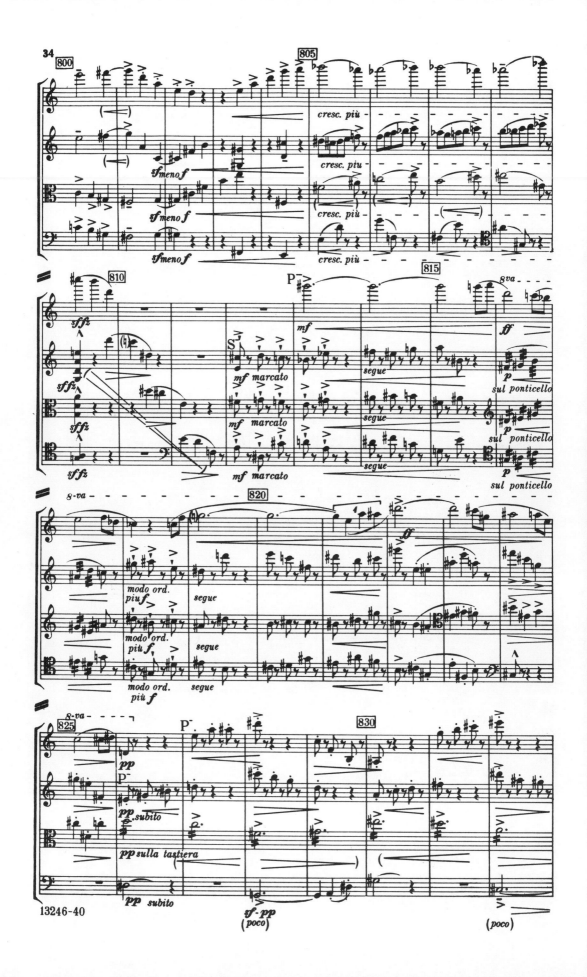

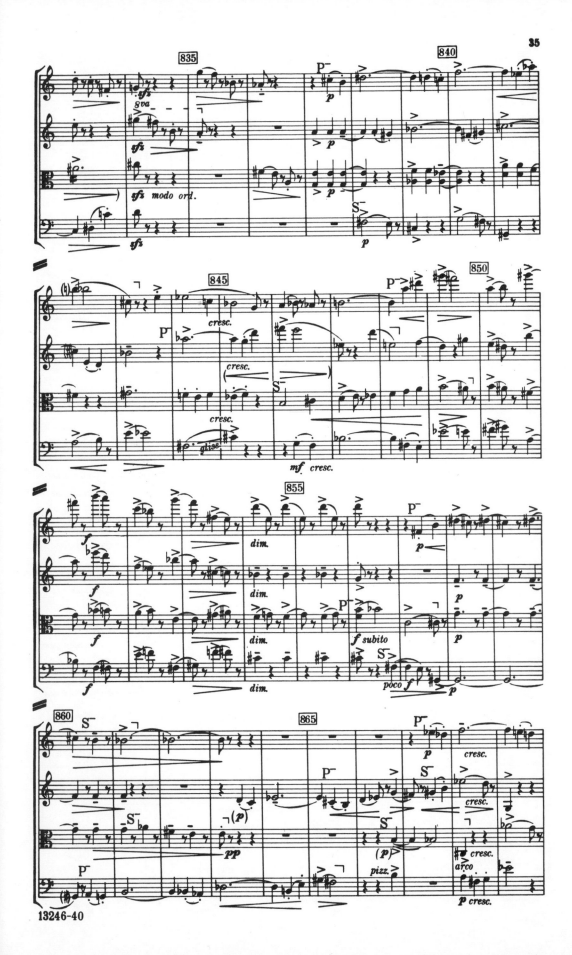

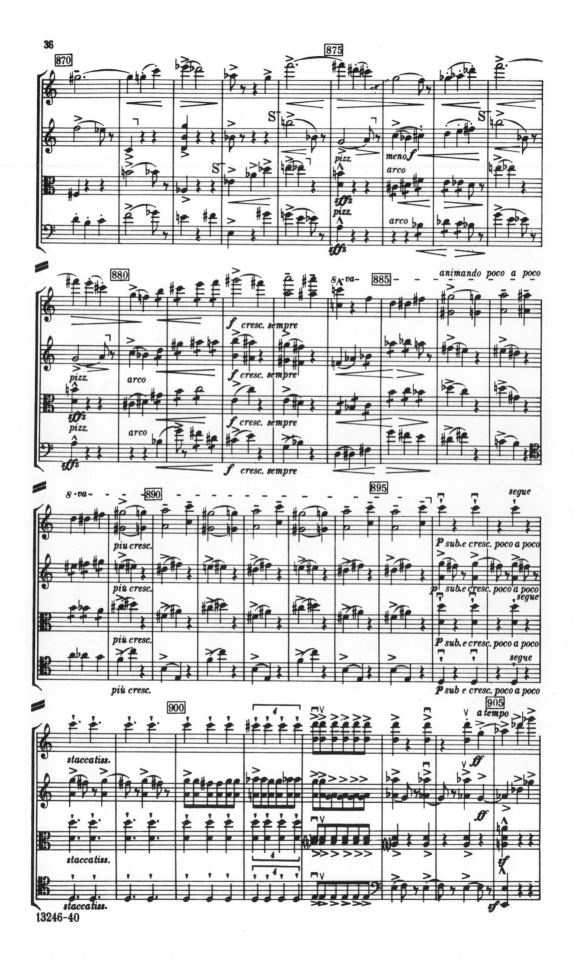

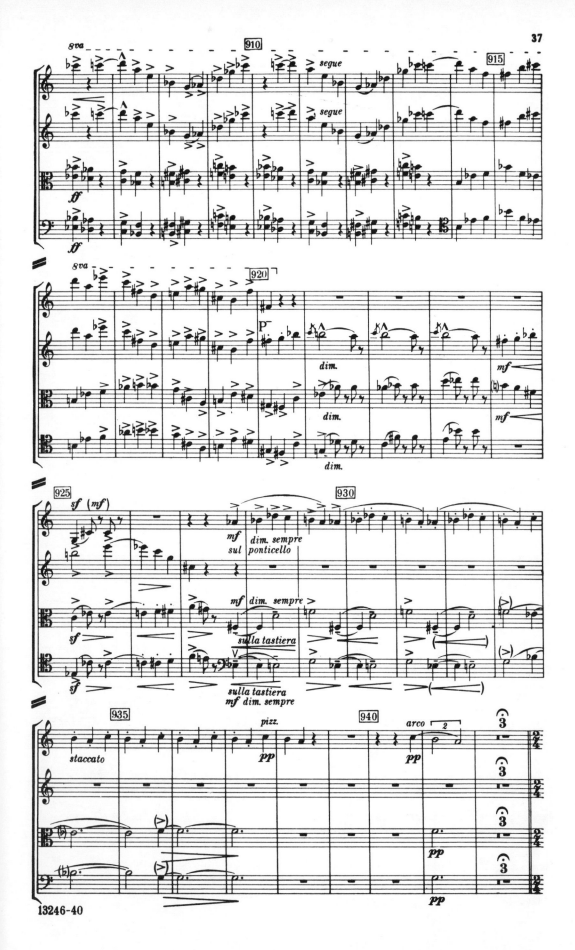

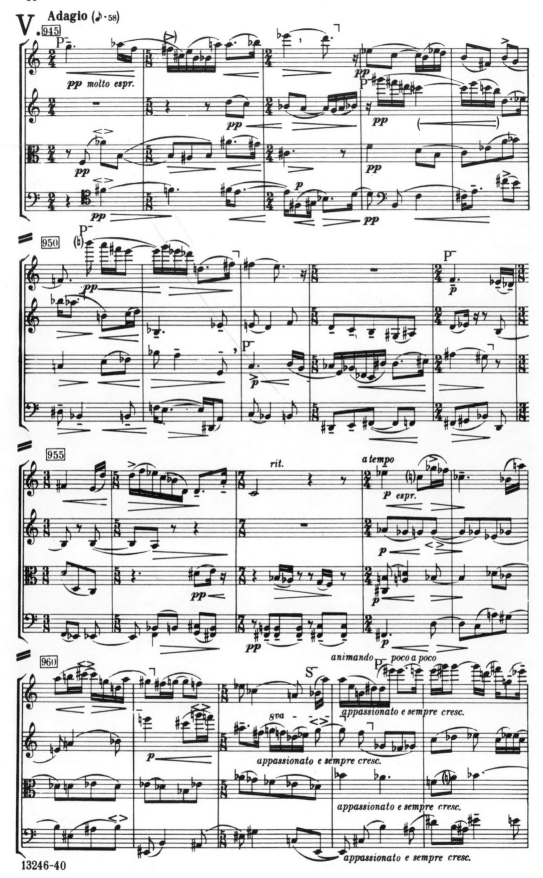

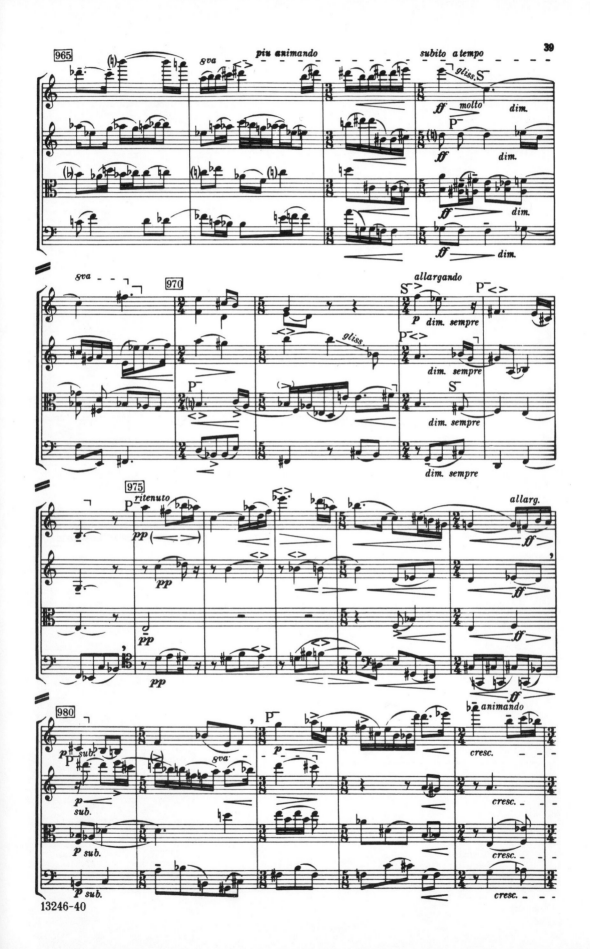

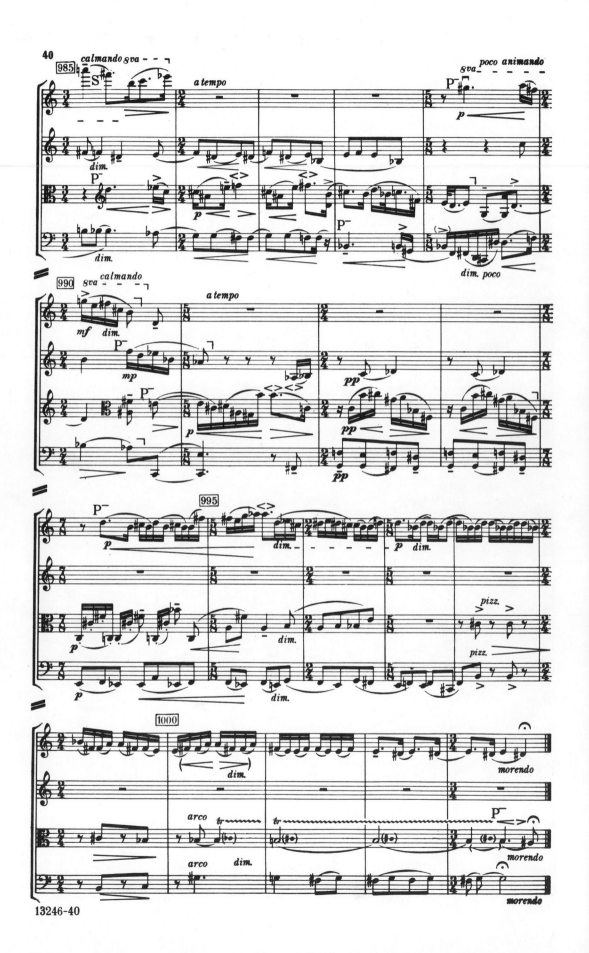

ISBN-13: 978-1-61774-140-1

Distributed By

HAL LEONARD

00220342

EXCLUSIVELY
DISTRIBUTED BY

HAL LEONARD

00220342